D0944713

Great Parties

SMART TALK

Great Parties:
How to Plan Them

Susan Wallach

Troll Associates

Library of Congress Cataloging-in-Publication Data

Wallach, Susan.
  Great parties, how to plan them / by Susan Wallach; illustrated
by Diana Magnuson.
    p.   cm.—(Smart talk)
  Summary: Presents plans for perfect parties, discussing
invitations to decorations, snacks to games.
  ISBN 0-8167-2291-9 (lib. bdg.)   ISBN 0-8167-2292-7 (pbk.)
  1. Children's parties—Juvenile literature. 2. Entertaining—
Juvenile literature. [1. Parties. 2. Entertaining.]
I. Magnuson, Diana, ill. II. Title. III. Series.
GV1205.W35 1991
793.2′1—dc20   90-46879

Table of Contents

It's Party Time!

*I*t's early November. School has been going on forever and you just know Thanksgiving vacation will never come. It's been great seeing all your friends back at school, but now you feel like all you do is homework, homework, homework. And you have eight more months of this! How can you possibly stand it?

Or it's August. You know you'll just melt if you touch anything. And the heat never stops. You love summer, but enough is enough. You need a break. What are you going to do?

1

Have a party!

So, it's not your birthday, and maybe there are no upcoming holidays to celebrate, but you don't need your birthday or holidays to have a party. A party can happen anytime for any reason!

And if it *is* your birthday, better still! You have a ready-made excuse for your own special celebration!

Uh-oh—here comes the hard part—perhaps you've never given a party before. You may have *had* parties, but maybe your parents did most of the planning and decision-making. They may have asked you what kind of cake you wanted or who you wanted to invite, but they basically took care of everything. You may not have even had a party that you remember (looking at pictures of yourself eating cake at the adorable age of three doesn't count).

So, congratulations. This may be the very first party that you're in charge of. Just deciding what kind of party to have, preparing for it and thinking about it can be lots of fun. Then, after all that, you still even get to have the party!

There are probably some of you who think giving a party is scary. Will everything go right? Will anyone come? Will everyone get along? Will they have fun? Will *you* have fun? Everyone from the first-time party-giver to experienced hostesses and caterers has those thoughts. Being nervous is allowed, but you shouldn't be petrified. Your party will be a success. We guarantee it! You just need to put in a little planning, ask for a little help from your family and friends (it's okay to get help from them; don't they ask you for help when they throw a party?) and, most importantly, have the desire to have a wonderful time!

2

USING THIS BOOK

While reading *Great Parties* and planning your party, you'll get to know three girls very well—Jasmine, Melissa and Ellen. Each of these girls is giving a specific kind of party and, depending on what you want your party to be like, you should pay attention to one of the girls more than the others. Each girl will make decisions and face problems that you might actually deal with while planning *your* party. And *Great Parties* will be with you every step of the way, from deciding what kind of party to have all the way through to cleaning up.

So, let your imagination run free and get ready to have a *great* party!

Selecting a Celebration

You know you want to have a party. Good. Now, the next thing to do is figure out what *kind* of party you want. You might already know that you want a backward party where everything is done backward (from your invitation to your clothing to the food—have your cake and eat it first). Or you might have a hint of an idea such as wanting everybody to dress up in crazy clothing. Or you might just know that you want to have a party where everybody has a good time (is there a better kind?).

The following quiz will help you figure out what kind of party you might be interested in having and which girl—Jasmine, Ellen or Melissa—is giving the kind of party that is closest to the kind you want to give.

☆☆ **PARTY-PLANNER QUIZ** ☆☆

For all quizzes, please write your answers on a separate sheet of paper.

1. *On vacation with your family, you like to:*
      a. Go to a summer cottage in a community where there are lots of other kids your age.
      b. Go camping in the summer or skiing in the winter—anywhere, as long as you can be outdoors.
      c. Visit museums and historic places in a city you've never been to before.
2. *You and your friends mostly:*
      a. Hang out together laughing, talking and seeing what happens.
      b. Do school sports or get together to play frisbee or softball.
      c. Go to movies, plays or exhibits.
3. *Your favorite types of movies are:*
      a. Comedies and love stories.
      b. Adventures and sweeping epics.
      c. Foreign films and dramas.
4. *The kind of women you admire are:*
      a. Known for their exciting and dramatic lives.
      b. Known for their adventurous spirits.
      c. Known for their inquiring minds.

5. *If you could travel back in time, you would be:*
    a. Queen Elizabeth and rule an empire.
    b. Sacajawea and explore the Western frontier.
    c. Marie Curie and make great scientific discoveries.
6. *The best party you ever went to was:*
    a. Your cousin's costume party when he invited fifty people, and everyone played different kinds of games, danced and laughed most of the time.
    b. Your older sister's birthday party when everyone went skating on the pond and then came back for lunch, hot chocolate and cake.
    c. When your friend's mother took six of you to the movies and then to a really nice restaurant for lunch afterward.
7. *When you get older, you want to be:*
    a. A ballerina, a spy, a movie star; anything and everything.
    b. A forest ranger, an agricultural consultant or an environmentalist.
    c. A scientist, a movie director or a college professor.

Count up the number of times you answered a, b or c.

If you chose mostly a's, your best bet would be to follow Jasmine's party through the book. Like you, Jasmine is extroverted, fun-loving and eager to try different things. She loves parties, enjoys being the center of attention and wants to be where the action is. Theme parties are probably best for you, so pay

Rollicking at the Roller Rink. Themes, like roller skating, make party planning fun!

special attention to the theme parties listed in Chapter Ten, then let your imagination run wild. You might want to dress up, or have a scavenger hunt, or create an adventure for your friends. A theme party can be anything and everything that fits your unique personality.

Outdoors is the place for those who picked mostly b's, so if that's you, Melissa is probably your soul mate. She's athletic, loves the outdoors and needs to be active all the time. Whether it's winter or summer, spring or fall, you love to be part of whatever nature has to offer. Being outdoors also gives you a feeling of freedom and adventure. You don't have to worry about being quiet or breaking things—you can be yourself. You like to do things and be active and alive. You like to play sports or games and have fun with a group of friends. Check out the outdoor parties in Chapter Ten and the outdoor games in Chapter Six.

For those of you who chose more c's, the whole world is yours to discover and Ellen is the girl to follow. She loves to curl up with a good book, watch an old movie or just hang out with one close friend. All of these activities suit your temperament just fine. Ellen loves to learn and discover, following intellectual pursuits. You too have many interests and enjoy exploring them. Pay attention to the activity parties, in which you can either share an activity you know and like with your friends (going to a museum, horseback riding, the planetarium), or you can all try something totally new.

Did you have a mix of a's, b's, and c's? That's okay, too. What are you in the mood for now? There may be something special you've wanted to do for a while, and this is the time to go for it. If you've wanted to go on adventure with your friends, then you might pick an activity party and follow Ellen. Or perhaps this is the time you want to go wild and a theme party would fit, so follow Jasmine. Or if this is your favorite season and you couldn't imagine being inside on such a special day, well then, go with Melissa and have fun in the great outdoors.

☆☆☆

Most importantly, plan a party that fits you and that you're happy with. Your party should reflect your personality, and you should have a good time at it. Now put on your party hat, sit back and get ready to have some fun!

PERTAINING TO PERMISSION

The next big step on the road to giving a party is discussing the whole idea with your parents and asking for their permission. This is one of the most important (if not THE most important) steps to planning a party. After all, without it, your party dreams are just that, dreams. Only your parents' permission can make these dreams come true.

Bringing up the topic might be difficult. If it's your birthday, the idea of a party may naturally come up. But if you want a party just because you know how much fun they are, the idea may come as a surprise to your parents, so don't be upset if they take some convincing.

If possible, before talking to your parents about it, you should have some idea as to the kind of party you want, where you want to have it, how many people you want to invite and what you want to do at the party—all the things we're going to talk about in the next chapter. You don't have to know all the answers, just enough to have a reasonable discussion. If all you really care about is having a party, suggest the idea to your parents and take it from there. Or you could lay each piece of the plan down, one by one, for them to consider.

Parents can be very helpful (really)! Having their help and support can mean the difference between no party at all and one of the greatest occasions of your life.

Party Particulars

"Hi, Julie, I have a great idea for a party," Jasmine said, talking on the phone to her best friend. "It's going to be a sixties party—you know, flower children, rock 'n' roll, tie-dyed shirts. I'm going to invite the whole class. It will be great."

PRE-PARTY POSERS

There are some basic questions you need to answer when planning a party, and we'll go over each one individually. These questions are:

1. What kind of party do you want?
2. How much room do you have?
3. What's your budget?
4. Who do you want to invite?
5. How will your family (parents, siblings, etc.) be involved?

WHAT KIND OF PARTY DO YOU WANT?

You've already taken the quiz and have some general idea as to what type of party you want to have. Now, let's get specific. That's what the rest of this book is for, planning the specifics of your party. Use Chapter Ten for different ideas, but feel free to pick and choose and come up with your own ideas as well. And no matter what type of party you decide on, remember that the main goal is to enjoy yourself, so don't take on too much. Just play it cool, you can always have another one. (And remember, if it's your birthday, it's easy enough to add a birthday cake to any party you choose.)

HOW BIG AND HOW MUCH?

Space and cost are important elements to consider when planning a party. Do you really have the room to fit, or the money to feed, 150 people? Do you really *know* 150 people?

Depending on the kind of party you're having, think about where you want the party. If you want a pool party, and you don't own a pool, you or one of your parents might make arrangements at the neighborhood swimming pool. If you love the small glass-enclosed porch in your house and want to have your party there, you'll have to invite fewer people. And if you want to play games, dance and be more active, then you'll probably need a bigger room or a short guest list.

If you're having a movie party in your home, where all you're doing is watching videos, then you can probably afford to invite a large number of people. But if you want to treat your friends to a day in the city and lunch, you may only be able to afford to invite four friends and not ten.

When food is the main focus of the party, your budget becomes a major concern. If you want to serve just chips and dips, you can probably afford to invite more friends than if you plan on serving a five-course meal. But if it's more important for you to have lots of people at your party, then you may choose to change the kind of food and make what you serve cheaper.

THE CAST OF CHARACTERS

Who to invite can be an extremely touchy question. Sometimes you want to invite everyone you know so there aren't any hurt feelings. But with some parties, there may not be room or it may be too expensive. Or you may decide to have a party with

15

only your camp friends or only your dancing-class friends, so it wouldn't be suitable to invite your hockey-team friends. Similarly, if you want your different friends to get to know each other, you may want to invite fewer guests so it's a quieter party and everybody has a chance to talk.

This is something you can discuss with your parents, a sister or brother or a good friend—someone who knows all the people involved. Remember: This is *your* party—do what makes you happy. Don't hurt anyone's feelings unnecessarily, but think about what you want and what you can do within the restrictions that space and money place on you. One rule: Never, never choose not to invite someone just to be cruel. You never know when the shoe could be on the other foot!

WHERE THE BOYS ARE

But what about boys?

The first thing to do is to decide whether you really *want* boys at your party or not. Here are some questions you can ask yourself to help you make up your mind:

- ✪ *Do you have friends who are boys?*
- ✪ *Is the group you hang out with made up of both girls and boys?*
- ✪ *What kind of party do you want to have? If it's a roller-skating party, why not invite boys? If it's a small afternoon tea, you might want to invite just girls.*
- ✪ *Will your parents allow you to have a boy/girl party?*
- ✪ *Will you have an equal or close to equal number of*

boys and girls? It might be uncomfortable for the one or two boys you invite if all the other guests are girls. Yet, there are plenty of boys who are comfortable being one of the few boys at a party filled with girls. Do what makes your friends feel comfortable.

Basically, if you want to and your parents say it's okay, go for it. And if you don't want to, or your parents don't want you to, don't worry about that either. Everybody will understand.

FAMILIES AND OTHER ATTENDEES

Families need special consideration, because most likely they are going to be there and the party may be held in their home. If you really don't want them to be involved, ask them politely and nicely if they would stay "behind the scenes" while your party is going on. Start by explaining that this is something you want to try to take care of on your own, but promise them that if anything starts to go wrong, you will get them immediately.

Keep in mind also that it might not be so bad to have them around. Maybe they'll even help out. They may choose to stay in the kitchen, help when you need them to and stay away when everything is fine. Or you may not mind if they hang around and visit with your friends for a while.

If you have brothers or sisters, do you want them to be involved? Depending on your relationship with them, your sister might be fun to have at your party, and your brother may be a help. If you know that is simply not the case, then talk to your parents in private. Explain to them that this is your special day or night, and you know that World World II would look like a picnic if you and your siblings were at the same party. Perhaps they could stay at a friend's house overnight or just for the day. Or if your siblings are older, ask your parents to talk with them so they understand that this is your party and they shouldn't interfere.

HELPFUL OR HORRENDOUS?

Handling your parents, brothers and sisters at a party is a delicate operation. Some of it depends on what everyone agreed upon before the party, but what if it was decided that your younger brother can stay and your parents will just help a little, and a little turns out to be too much? Take the following quiz and find out how well you can handle families at functions.

☆☆　　FAMILY QUIZ　　☆☆

1. *Your mom said she would let you handle everything, but when you go into the kitchen to get more bags of chips, you see that she already took them out and put them in bowls. You:*
   a. Storm into her bedroom, screaming that she never lets you do anything.
   b. Refuse to use them since you didn't get them ready.
   c. Thank her and bring the chips down to the party.
   d. Go into her room, weeping tears of gratitude.

2. *You asked your father to take pictures at your party, but he hasn't taken one picture yet and the party is half over. You:*
   a. Fling the camera across the room.
   b. Don't smile or even look at him when he finally begins to shoot.
   c. Remind him quietly that he promised to take pictures.
   d. Understand that he's probably not in the mood and decide that memories are just as good as photos.
3. *There are thirteen guests at your party, and only three of them are boys! The boys were so uncomfortable at first that you thought they might leave. But then your older brother and one of his friends showed up, and now the boys seem to be having a good time. You:*
   a. Remind your brother and his friends that it's your party and they weren't invited.
   b. Ignore any friend who talks to your brother.
   c. Do nothing, but relax and enjoy your party, thanking your brother later.
   d. Tell your brother you will be his slave for a year.
4. *Your older sister has been great—she even lent you her favorite sweater—but now she's being even more helpful and organizing the games: You:*
   a. Announce loudly that it's your sister's party, not yours anymore.
   b. Refuse to play or do anything else.
   c. Wait until she's finished and, while the game is going on, thank her and politely ask her to let you organize the rest of the games.

19

d. Thank her profusely, realizing that she can do a better job than you can.
5. *You decided to have a skating party. You discover your brother and his friends at the rink, and they're deliberately bumping into your friends. You:*
   a. Tell one of the guards that he's dangerous and pretend he isn't your brother no matter what he says.
   b. Make all your friends stop skating until he leaves.
   c. Ask your mother or father to tell your brother to stop bothering you and your friends.
   d. Skate with your brother and buy him candy.

☆☆☆

Now see how many times you picked a, b, c or d. If you picked mostly a's, you need to learn how to control your temper—it will only get you into more trouble and won't help take care of the problem. You'll also create a scene, which could spoil your party.

Choosing b, although less harsh and abrupt, doesn't really take care of the problem at hand. Usually you're not really accomplishing anything, and you'll bring your party to a complete stop. You might want to think of your friends before you do that.

If you picked more c's, then you are able to keep a level head and effectively take care of the problem or appreciate when someone is helping you. You don't get upset even if your party isn't going exactly as you planned. Keeping your sense of humor helps you keep the party mood and helps enable you to accomplish what you want.

If you picked more d's than the other choices, then you should get an award for Wimp of the Week. There is no reason to let people walk all over you in an effort to be sweet and good.

☆☆☆

In general, try to size up each situation and see if it's really necessary to say something or just let it be. Follow your instincts, but don't create a big fuss. If you need to talk to someone about a problem, do it quietly and not in front of everyone. And if you have to deal with a brother or a sister, it's better to ask your parents to say something instead of trying to strong-arm him or her out of the room.

PARTY CHECK LIST—Pre-Party Questions

Use this list to make sure you've planned out the basics of your party:
1. What kind of party do you want to have?
2. Have you received permission from your parents?
3. Whom do you want to invite? Everyone? A select few?
4. How many guests *can* you invite because of space and cost?
5. What about your parents, brothers and sisters?

JASMINE THINKS BIG

All three of our "party girls" had to talk to their parents to work out if they could have a party, what kind of party to have, the guest list and what to do with brothers, sisters and even parents during the party.

Jasmine thought it might be a bit difficult to get her parents' approval. But she had several things already in her favor: She knew what kind of party she wanted—a sixties party. She also knew who she wanted to invite—her whole class. And she knew that she *didn't* want her younger brother to be anywhere near her party.

When Jasmine talked to her mother and father, they were easily convinced for the most part: It was clear she had really thought the matter through, and they were excited because they loved the sixties. But when Jasmine said she wanted to invite everyone from her class, her parents just didn't see how they could fit twenty-five kids in the living room. Eighteen was the limit, which was stretching it according to her mother.

Jasmine's mother suggested only inviting the girls, but Jasmine wanted everyone to come so no one would feel left out. Besides, a lot of her friends were boys and she wanted them at her party.

Then Jasmine had an idea. Why not clean up the basement? There would be enough room down there if some of the family's junk was moved out of the way. Jasmine offered to clean the whole area and get it ready. That way she could have the party she wanted, and her family would have one less nasty job to do during spring cleaning. Her parents agreed and her father even offered to help.

At first, Jasmine's mother said that Jasmine's little brother Danny had to be at the party; he *was* her brother, after all. But Jasmine pointed out that Danny was usually such a pain around her friends that it aggravated her parents as well as her. So Jasmine asked if he could spend the evening at a friend's house, and her mother agreed.

Then they started to plan the party itself. Jasmine's father and mother both offered to help Jasmine figure out what to wear, and donated some of their posters and knickknacks from the sixties for her party. It would be more difficult bringing the food downstairs from the kitchen, but her mother didn't mind.

Jasmine wanted to have dancing, but she knew some of the boys in her class would be uncomfortable dancing, so she thought of a way to make it easier for everyone. Since there would be an equal number of boys and girls, she would write down famous couples, each name on a different piece of paper. She had a girl pile and a boy pile, and when her guests came in, each person would have to pick one from the correct pile. Some of the couples were Romeo and Juliet, Rhett and Scarlet, Napoleon and Josephine. When she wanted the dancing to start, she would tell everyone to find their partner and dance the first two dances with that person. This way, she would get everyone to start dancing and break the ice.

She also wanted to get everyone to paint their own face or someone else's with flowers and stars

Try face painting at a groovy sixties party.

like they did in the sixties. Her parents said she could buy face paint and inexpensive makeup brushes.

MELISSA CELEBRATES OUTSIDE

Melissa's birthday is in January, but she had always wanted a picnic birthday party. She was sick for her birthday this year and wanted to celebrate it in the spring. Talking to her best friend, Diane, Melissa decided she'd like to have a party in the park near her home, with lots of friends, volleyball games, rowing on the lake and plenty of food.

Melissa's mom was all for a spring party for her daughter. Her birthday was also in the winter and she, too, had always wanted to celebrate outdoors. There were a few problems though. Melissa's mom was nervous about the rowing. Volleyball and other games sounded fine, but the girls in boats on their own worried her. She couldn't watch over all of them, even with an additional chaperon, and so she said no to the boating idea.

Melissa decided to invite only the girls on her hockey team and three of her favorite cousins. She liked a few boys in her class, but she knew her mother would be more comfortable with a girls-only party.

The last problem was food. How were Melissa and her mother going to cook enough food for everyone and get everything to the park? Since her mom worked all week, the weekends were her only free time, and Melissa's father lived two thousand miles away. Besides, feeding all those people was expensive. Melissa's mother thought of having a potluck picnic, where each girl has to bring a dish. That way the work would be shared; Melissa and her mom would do a lot of the work, but all the girls would feel like they participated in creating a great picnic lunch. Melissa loved the idea.

ELLEN BECOMES THEATRICAL

Ellen's birthday was coming up and she wanted to celebrate it in a special way, preferably in a way that involved the theater. She and her father came up with the idea of going to a play at the small theater company a few towns away. Ellen and her friends could see the play and then come back for dinner or cake at her apartment.

Ellen loved the idea and wanted to invite her five close friends from school and four of her theater camp friends, but her father said that it would be too expensive to pay for nine girls. Five was the limit.

Ellen agreed and called up the theater. She found out that her first choice, Saturday, which was her actual birthday, was sold out, but there were tickets for the Sunday matinee. There were even seats next to each other. Ellen reserved seven seats for her five school friends, herself and her father.

After making the reservations, Ellen realized she would have to alter her party somewhat. Instead of a dinner, her friends would come over for lunch, go to the play and then return to the apartment for cake.

Inviting Invitations

*E*llen and her father were in the fourth card store of the day, looking for invitations. None of them was just right, and Ellen could tell her father was getting annoyed.

"I know," Ellen said suddenly, "I'll make my own invitations. I have the perfect idea."

INVITATIONAL ETIQUETTE

Before you start writing out your invitations, you have a couple of decisions to make; specifically, *when* and *how* are you going to tell your friends about your party? *When* is important because you need to give your friends time to receive and respond to the invitations. And once you know who is coming, you'll need time to plan your party food-wise and activity-wise.

How is more a matter of style. Some people like to mail their invitations, and others like to hand them out. It's entirely up to you. Would it be more fun to give them to your friends or know that they'll receive them in the mail? Are you inviting some friends and not others? If so, it may be kinder not to hand them out in front of everyone.

Of course, if you're in a rush, you can always call your friends and tell them about your party. If you do, it's a good idea to write all the information down and have that list in front of you when you call, so you don't leave anything out. If you need to know whether your friend is coming or not, be sure to make that clear. One plus about written invitations is that your guest will have a reminder of when and where the party is. A phone call is more casual and a lot quicker, but you might want to make sure that everyone gets an invitation as well.

However you choose to inform your guests, don't forget to tell them if there is something special about the party, like if it has a theme, or if it's a surprise for someone or if they should bring gifts for exchang-

Let your fingers do the walking when you throw a last minute get-together.

ing. (Because if everyone but your friend Suzanne comes in costume, she'll feel just horrible.) If you are having a grab bag, make sure everyone brings a gift and be sure to give them a spending limit. If it's a surprise party, you have to include that information on the invitation or else the guest of honor will find out.

Use the check list below to make sure your invitation is complete.

Invitation Check List

1. Who's giving the party.
2. What kind of party it is—birthday, surprise, slumber, costume and so on.
3. Where it's being held—include directions if necessary.
4. When it's being held—date and time it begins and ends.
5. Your phone number, so your guests can call and tell you if they're coming or not.
6. Any special information—do they need to dress in a certain way, bring something or prepare anything ahead of time?

★★★

MAKING YOUR OWN INVITATIONS

You start designing your party from the moment you choose your invitations, so if you have the time, why not create them yourself? Homemade invitations have a personal feel which makes them much nicer than the ones you buy in a store, and they're a lot cheaper too!

Here are some hints for designing your own invitations. First, always suit your invitation to the kind of party you're having:

- *If you're having a movie party, you can call it a screening and write the invitation as though you're a big Hollywood producer.*
- *If you're having a games party, create a mini board game and have the party information on different squares.*
- *For a mystery party, try making a ransom-note invitation by cutting out the letters from magazines and newspapers.*
- *If you're having a birthday party, you can copy your birth certificate and paste the copies on the front of your invitation. Or you could use a baby photo instead. If you're having a Fourth of July party, use sparkles and shiny confetti in the invitation, so when your friends open it, they are showered with glitter.*

Making invitations in different shapes to carry out the theme of your party is very simple and looks great:

- *If you're having a mystery party, cut your invitation in the shape of a dead body.*
- *If you're having a beach party, cut construction paper in the shape of a beach umbrella or seashell.*
- *For a Halloween party, try making invitations shaped like pumpkins, cats or witches.*

31

You can also use materials other than paper:

✪ *Blow up a balloon, write all the information on the balloon with a permanent marker or a felt-tip pen, let it dry and then let all the air out. (When you mail the balloons to your friends, you might want to include a slip of paper that says, "Blow me up.")*

✪ *Write the invitation on a wide ribbon and roll it up, tying it up with another thinner ribbon. Your friends have to unroll it to read about your party.*

Almost anything is possible—just use your imagination and have fun!

AN ELEGANT INVITATION

Ellen set to work on her invitations immediately because she needed to confirm the reservations for the play two weeks in advance. She decided to make her invitations resemble a theater program. She folded her typing paper as though it were a book and then typed out each page.

Ellen's Birthday
(A play in three acts)
Directed by Ellen Conover
Starring Ellen Conover

Act I: An elegant noon meal at Ellen's home
        (487 Clinton Place, Apt. 3Q)
Intermission
Act II: Later that same day at the theater

32

Intermission
Act III: That evening, back at Ellen's home.

All acts take place on Sunday, April 28, starting at twelve o'clock noon.
Please R.S.V.P. 555-5840 no later than April 15.
Dress will be appropriate for the theater.

SIMPLY SIXTIES

Jasmine had tons of schoolwork and lots of invitations to write, so she decided not to do anything very fancy. Instead, she bought a bunch of postcards with pictures having something to do with the sixties—such as the Beatles, the Kennedys, flowers or Andy Warhol paintings—and wrote the party information on the back.

Groovy, Cool, Hip!

Calling all friends—
Jasmine's having a sixties party!
Where: Jasmine's house—3 Stanley Road (call for directions)
When: May 5 from 8:00 to 11:00 P.M.
R.S.V.P. 555-5163

Dress in sixties clothes—leather-fringed vests, tie-dyed clothes, moccasins, beads, flowers, headbands and work shirts.

Be there or be square!

Jasmine handed out the invitations to her friends in school three weeks before the actual party, so they would keep that evening free and have time to work on their outfits.

THE INVITING OUTDOORS

Melissa chose to make her invitations by cutting out black-and-white pictures, cartoons, words and phrases from magazines and gluing them onto a white piece of paper, which she then photocopied. All the pictures had to do with picnics, being outside and various sports and games. Before copying the invitation, she included all the information her friends would need.

It's my birthday—five months later

Come celebrate in the great outdoors
When: May 12th (rain or shine)
     1 - 5 P.M.
Where: Verona Park (call for directions), then
       follow the balloons
R.S.V.P. 555-2068 by May 5

What to bring—It's a potluck picnic so when you call to R.S.V.P., tell me what kind of food you want to bring.

Melissa handed most of the invitations to her teammates at a practice three weeks before the twelfth. Then she mailed the others to her cousins.

Food, Glorious Food

"I'm so glad you can come, Holly. You want to make a salad? Terrific!" Melissa exclaimed on the phone. Now she had most of the food taken care of. All she needed were two more people to bring soda and juice.

TO COOK OR NOT TO COOK

The following quiz will help you decide whether to devote time and effort preparing a gourmet meal for your guests, or whether you should just open a bag of chips instead.

☆☆ THE FOOD AND YOU QUIZ ☆☆

1. *When the recipe calls for a teaspoon, you:*
    a. Pull out the measuring spoons and pick the one that reads "1 tsp."
    b. Get the spoon you just used for your tea.
    c. Close the book and wing it.
2. *Finger sandwiches:*
    a. Are tiny sandwiches.
    b. Are rolled up slices of baloney, made to look like fingers.
    c. Sound disgusting; besides, you're a vegetarian.
3. *When a recipe calls for beating an egg:*
    a. You crack the egg into a bowl and blend the yolk and the white together.
    b. You ask your mom to do it.
    c. You take an egg and slap it around.
4. *The stove:*
    a. Is your favorite appliance. (The washing machine is another story.)
    b. Has burners on top and an oven.
    c. Stove shmove—can it make music?
5. *You prefer to:*
    a. Make your own breakfast of French toast, juice and fruit.

b. Have someone cook a delicious meal for you.

c. Get a slice of cold pizza and run.

6. *You go into the kitchen:*

a. About ten times a day, because you love to help prepare meals.

b. On your way to the dining room to eat.

c. There's a kitchen in this house?

7. *At your party the most important part is:*

a. The food.

b. Having a good time and eating well.

c. Being with your friends.

It probably isn't too hard to figure out how to keep score. Just count up the times you answered with a, b or c.

If you answered mostly with a's, you are practically one with the kitchen. If you choose to have a dinner party, you'll do just fine. It's okay to ask for help, though; there's no reason to do everything yourself. And although food is important and fun, so are the other parts of your party—do plan a few simple activities other than eating.

If most of your answers were b's, maybe the kitchen isn't exactly familiar territory. You don't seem to know a whole lot about cooking, so it probably wouldn't be a good idea to tackle a six-course meal for your party. Simple packaged foods that you can tear open and pour out into bowls or microwave seem about your speed. If you do choose to try something more complex, make sure you get help—and lots of it!

If you chose mostly c's, you really don't care about

food or cooking. You probably wouldn't even notice if the kitchen disappeared one day! For you, too, simple foods with little or no preparation are all that is necessary. One bit of advice: Do serve *something*! Parties tend to make people hungry.

You might be a mix of all the letters. For this party, what are you in the mood for? Do you want to put in some special effort and make the food a bit fancier? Or are other elements of your party more important to you? If the idea of making something that your friends will actually have to eat scares you, or if this party will be happening when you have a zillion other obligations in the same week, don't get all worked up about food. See the section on finger food below and *think simple*! Your party and all the planning should be fun, not frightening.

☆☆☆

FINGER FOODS BY THE HANDFUL

The main ingredients in party food are simplicity, convenience and lack of mess. With basic party food, you can put everything out before your guests arrive. Then all you have to do is make sure the bowls and platters stay filled. (You can ask your friends or parents to help with that in case you need to take care of other things during the party.) Pretzels, potato chips, popcorn and candies are traditional party favorites, but there are other snacks that are just as quick and simple.

Here are some ideas for party food that are easy, filling and much healthier than junk food:

- ✪ *Cut-up vegetables and dip*
- ✪ *Cheese and crackers*
- ✪ *Spreads like hummus or even peanut butter*
- ✪ *Cut-up fruit or bowls of dried fruit*
- ✪ *Tortilla chips with salsa or guacamole*

FOOD ONLY, PLEASE

Your entire party can be centered around food, but if you do intend to prepare a full meal, make that the focus of the party. A sit-down meal, plus dancing and a lot of games might be too much to handle and take too long to set up.

A really easy way to have food be the center of the party without having to cook or spend a lot of money is to make it potluck. Potluck means that each one of your guests brings a prepared dish. You can give each guest a broad category—such as dessert or vegetables—or you can be more specific.

If you decide to do it all yourself, there are certain foods that are easier to prepare when you are entertaining many people. Lasagna is good because you can make it the day before and then just heat it up. A big bowl of pasta and sauce is another favorite, and you can make your own sauce in advance. Baked chicken is easy too—just let it cook while you hang out with your friends.

If you do have a meal party, make sure you schedule it so you can spend time with your friends and not be stuck in the kitchen the whole time. This may be the kind of party where you'll want help from your parents.

Here are some additional ideas for a food-centered party:

- ✪ *A create-your-own-sundae party*
- ✪ *A bake-out where your friends help make cookies or cake*
- ✪ *A breakfast party where you all help make pancakes or waffles*
- ✪ *A barbecue*

PERFECT PRESENTATIONS

Whether you're having a sit-down meal or just snacks, the way you serve the food adds to the festive air of the party. Little touches such as serving chips in a glass or pottery bowl make the chips more inviting and the room more attractive.

You don't need to go bananas over this—and you certainly don't need to buy a lot of fancy plates and platters. Just use your imagination and have fun!

PICNIC FOOD

For her picnic, Melissa and her mother decided they should bring the main courses, but everyone else would bring the other supplies—it would be a potluck picnic. Melissa drew up a list of the foods she wanted, and when her friends called they dis-

40

cussed what would be fun to have at a picnic. Her final list of foods and who would bring them looked like this:

1. Hamburgers, hot dogs and dessert   Melissa
2. Buns and rolls   Diane
3. Mustard and catsup   Cindi
4. Sandwiches   Cecelia and Shari
5. Salad   Ruby and Holly
6. Potato salad   Rose and Lisa
7. Potato chips   Roberta
8. Pickles and relish   Penny
9. Fruit   Jessica
10. Sodas and juices   Michelle, Emma and Madeline

PARTY FOOD CLASSICS

Jasmine knew that she didn't want to fuss over food at her party at all. She decided to have easy things but lots of them: chips and dip, cut-up vegetables, candy, sodas and juices, some cheese and crackers, brownies and chocolate chip cookies. She planned it so her mother wouldn't have to run up and down the stairs getting lots of extra food—it could all be stored downstairs.

SIMPLY DELICIOUS

Ellen and her father planned a simple lunch. They would have melon, honey-mustard chicken breast with salad and rice, and then birthday cake after the play.

They planned to work together. Ellen's sister promised to make the salad that morning and put it in the refrigerator until it was time to eat. Ellen would set the table and cut up the melon while her father took care of the chicken and rice.

At the meal, Ellen and her friends would sit down to eat the melon while her father kept an eye on the chicken and rice. They'd serve the chicken, salad and rice to her friends, and would both sit down to eat with them.

As soon as lunch was over they would leave for the play. Ellen's sister, who had a research paper to finish and couldn't go to the play, would reset the table for dessert.

Ellen thought it sounded perfect.

Designing Your Party

"Julie," Jasmine said to her best friend between classes, "you have to come over on Friday night and help me decorate the basement for the party."

"How are you going to decorate it?"

"I'm not sure yet." Jasmine answered. "What do you think of when you think of the sixties? My parents have some stuff, but I don't want this to be just any old party."

DRESS UP YOUR PARTY

Music and decorations give your party atmosphere—the feeling that this event is special. Decorations can give the room a general feeling of festivity or one which is specific to the kind of party you're throwing. Music is great for dancing, of course, and also for creating certain moods.

When trying to decide how to decorate, keep in mind the kind of party you are throwing. Do you really need to go all out with decorations? Maybe putting up some streamers is enough. But if you do decide you want lots of decorations, ask yourself the following questions:

1. How much time will you have before the party, either that day or the night before, to buy the decorations and put them up?
2. Do decorations fit in your budget? If not, can you create the look you want with the supplies you have at home?
3. Are decorations important enough for you to buy them with some of the money budgeted for food or favors?

Once you've worked out the answers to these questions, you'll be ready to begin thinking of decorating ideas. Keep in mind that there are probably a lot of things in your house or apartment that will transform an ordinary room into a party room.

DECORATING OPTIONS

When you are thinking about how you want the room to look, let your imagination go wild. First come up with the great ideas, and then figure out how to make them work financially and physically. Here are some ideas just to get you started:

- *If you are having a luau, do you imagine palm trees? Your parents may own potted plants or small trees that you could use.*
- *Do you want a spooky look for your Halloween party? Get old sheets and drape them over all the furniture, to make it look like a haunted house. You can also get inexpensive fake "cobwebs" in most joke shops, and you can also cut out "ghost footprints" from black construction paper and tack them across the floor and up a wall or two.*
- *Are you throwing a graduation party and you want to remember all the good times you've shared with your friends? Get their photos starting from kindergarten through last year, paste them to a board and hang it up. Get your class photos and include them. If you have an instant camera, leave room for a picture of all of you taken at the party.*

Lighting has a lot to do with atmosphere. Turning out most of the lights and stringing up simple, white Christmas-tree lights along the ceiling or around doorways can help transform a boring living room into a new, mysterious setting. (If there is a mirror in the room, string the lights around it as well.) Cov-

45

ering the lamp shades with a light fabric in bright colors will make the room look immensely festive. (Important note: Make sure you don't put fabric over the top of a lamp shade; always wrap it *around* the shade itself. Putting it over the top could cause a fire.)

One thing to remember is that a little decoration will go a long way. You don't need to overwhelm a room to give it a party air. Just changing the lighting or adding streamers or balloons will do a lot.

MIX-AND-MATCH MUSIC

Music helps with creating atmosphere, too. You might want to have music playing the entire time. If you do, put on softer music for the beginning of the party when your friends are first arriving. This way they can hang out and talk and not have to compete with the music. You'll probably want to turn it off if you're playing games, but once the dancing starts, turn the music up higher!

Recording your favorite songs on tape is a good way to keep the music flowing. With tapes all you have to be aware of is changing them every so often. If you're playing albums, or even CDs (unless you have a programmable audio system changer), you'll have to get up more often to get the mix you want. A homemade tape can keep going for at least forty-five minutes at a time if you buy ninety-minute tapes.

It can be really fun to make your own tape. It takes time—time to figure out what you want, time to change the record, time to play each song—but

*Pick out the songs you want ahead of time and make your
own dance tape so you can enjoy the music when it's party
time.*

when you're finished, you'll have your own personal party tape.

If you're having a theme party, you might want to stick to a certain style of music. But theme party or no, you can always add your personal favorites. You don't *have* to listen to Don Ho all night at a luau.

You also don't have to have any music at all. It just may not be right for your slumber or Halloween party or you may have enough activities planned so that music wouldn't really be necessary.

FAVORS TO GO

In medieval times, a lady or even a prince would give a "favor" to a particular friend or knight. These favors, or gifts, were often ribbons, gloves or other such special things to show their regard. By the late sixteenth century, those who received such favors were called "favorites," and sometimes received lavish gifts of land or money from the king or queen.

Today, favors are often given at birthday parties to thank the guests who have brought birthday presents for the hostess. You don't need to be a queen— or to have a royal treasury for buying gifts. It's fun to give an inexpensive favor that is connected to the party or to you. For instance, if you:

- ✪ *Are having a candle-making party, everyone can bring home a candle.*
- ✪ *Are celebrating with a swim party, buy cheap, crazy sunglasses or beach balls for everyone.*
- ✪ *Know how to make origami figures; you can either*

make some for everyone, or buy little origami kits and have your guests make their own origami favors during the party.

If your budget isn't big enough to buy favors and you desperately want to give them out, it's possible to come up with gifts that won't cost a lot. Do you love to bake? If it's a winter party, make your favorite gingerbread cookies. If you have beautiful handwriting or can do calligraphy, make a name card for each friend. Just think about what you can do and like to do, and you're sure to come up with an inexpensive but very personal favor.

And remember—it's not necessary to give favors at your party. It's a traditional and polite thing to do, but if it doesn't fit into your budget or you have too many guests, don't feel you have to give a gift. Your friends are coming to celebrate *your* party with *you* and have fun, not to add another favor to their collection.

SCALED-DOWN DECORATIONS

Ellen decided not to do anything to her living room and dining room. She wanted elegance, and she thought the rooms were elegant enough as they were. She simply put a bouquet of fresh flowers on the table, and her father agreed to let her light some candles at dessert time. Ellen taped some of her favorite classical pieces of music to play during lunch and dessert, but decided not to have music for opening her presents. Basically, she wanted a day that felt very grown-up and simple.

Although Ellen didn't do anything special in the way of decorating, she did create an atmosphere of elegance through her choice of flowers, candles and music.

IT'S A FESTIVAL!

Melissa, on the other hand, wanted giant balloons and ribbons *everywhere*. One purpose for the balloons and ribbons was so that her friends would know where her picnic site was. In addition, she wanted the most festive-looking area she could create. She and her mother bought inexpensive ribbons at a fabric store to tie around the trees in the park. They bought big and colorful balloons to attach to the ribbons, the picnic tables, low branches—anywhere they could reach. The tablecloths, paper plates and cups they bought were all primary colors—red, blue and yellow.

Melissa thought about bringing music, but decided she didn't want to disturb the other people in the park.

She decided to give away party favors since her friends were being nice enough to help by bringing food. She and her mother found a store where they bought pretty but inexpensive kites. Her guests would be able to fly them at the picnic.

EMPHASIZING THE EAST

Jasmine didn't know what to do to create the feeling of the sixties. She had the music all figured out—her father helped her make tapes from his old albums, so she had dance and non-dance tapes—but the decorations were giving her problems. She had some posters of the Beatles and other sixties rock 'n' roll stars, but most of them wouldn't mean anything to her friends. If she added streamers and balloons, it just wouldn't look sixties.

Then her mother remembered the Far Eastern things she used to furnish her room during the sixties. She helped Jasmine attach an Indian cotton bedspread to the basement ceiling so it made the room look like the inside of a tent. Jasmine took the old throw pillows that her mother had all over the house and brought them downstairs for people to sit on.

Because the overhead light was hidden by the cotton spread, they brought down some lamps and covered the shades with a light fabric. Jasmine also bought blue light bulbs, which changed the lighting in the room even more. Suddenly the basement was transformed into a room of mystery. Jasmine's mother suggested that she burn incense the day before and the morning of the party so the room would have a more exotic smell.

Jasmine loved the end result!

Of the three girls, Melissa spent the most money on decorations for her party because she had to buy all the paper plates and cups as well as balloons and ribbons, while Ellen and Jasmine mainly used what was in their homes. But it took all of them lots of time to come up with the look they wanted and then actually achieve it.

51

Games to Go By

What do you think of when you hear the words "party games"? Kid stuff, right? Pin-the-Tail-on-the-Donkey and Telephone? Well, there's a lot more to party games than just that. What exactly are your guests going to do while they are at your party? Will they dance? Will they tell stories? Will they play volleyball? All these activities are games of a sort, so they require some planning.

There are all kinds of games you can choose from. Some parties are more quiet than others, and certain types of games fit that mood. But if you're having an outdoor party, for example, relay races are probably better than word games.

The following is a list of various games you might want to play at your party. It is divided into three different categories—physical, semi-physical and quiet. A lot of these games can be competitive, but it's best to play them just for fun, whether they're volleyball, Charades or Killer. You don't want anyone to be upset because she or he lost—games are for having a good time, not judging who is the best or worst at something.

If teams have to be selected, it's a good idea to have them picked from a hat. If you have twenty people, write BLUE on ten pieces of paper and RED on the other ten. (Have blue and red scarves or caps on hand so players can tell who is on which team.) Everyone takes a piece of paper out of a hat or box, and that's how the teams are created. If you have a game that requires groups of two or three, use as many colors, numbers or letters as you need to create the teams. This is also a great way to get your guests to mix and spend time with people they don't know very well.

A HINT

If you're playing games at your party, make sure you have everything organized beforehand. You don't want to have to hunt for rolls of toilet paper for Wrap-the-Mummy when you could be with your friends. Collect everything you'll need in the days before the party and store it somewhere close at hand.

PHYSICAL GAMES

These games are good for playing outdoors, since you'll have more room. If you do choose to play some of them indoors, make sure you have removed any breakables from the area and that you have everyone help clean up.

WRAP-THE-MUMMY

Ask your guests to form two-person teams. One person is the mummy and the other is the wrapper. Give each team one or two rolls of toilet paper. The object of the race is to be the first team to wrap the mummy up so that no clothing or skin shows. A team could say they are finished, but if there is skin showing, they are not the winners. Also, tell people to cover the mummy's nose and mouth last, and with only one layer of toilet paper. Live "mummies" need to breathe! Breaking out of the toilet paper is great fun but also messy: Get everyone to help you clean up.

MARCO POLO

Marco Polo is Blind Man's Buff played in a pool. Everyone gets in the shallow end of a pool and one person, "It," is blindfolded. "It" calls out "Marco" and everyone else answers "Polo." This goes on until It finds and tags someone, who then becomes the next It.

VOLLEYBALL, FRISBEE, SOFTBALL AND SWIMMING

You know how to play these! Just have a great time and remember that winning is not the important thing.

SEMI-PHYSICAL GAMES

These games are perfect for either inside or outdoors. Semi-physical means you're not just sitting with a pencil, but you're not running a relay race either. It's somewhere in between.

PAPER BAG DRAMATICS

Divide your guests into groups of three or four. Give each group a bag filled with four or five items that you find in your home. (Note: Don't use anything that is valuable or precious to you.) Each group goes into a separate corner or area and makes up a short skit using all the items. Then each group performs their skit for the rest. One bag could hold a water pistol, a paperback book, a pipe, a bandage and a seashell. The items shouldn't be related to each other—you wouldn't put a water pistol, a policeman's badge, a Swiss army knife, rope and fake money in the same bag because that would make it too easy! Also, the items can be used as what they are, or as something else that is similarly shaped. For example, the pipe could be a pipe or the receiver of a telephone.

CHARADES

An old-time favorite that is still a lot of fun. Make sure everyone knows how to play and knows the gestures for everything (tugging on your ear means "sounds like," three fingers against your arm means there are three syllables and so on). Divide into teams and time how long it takes for a team to guess the song or movie title or whatever a person on the other team is silently acting out. Or everyone can play together and try to guess at the same time. Whoever guesses correctly gets to perform the next charade.

KILLER

Have a deck of playing cards on hand, and take out one card for each player. Make sure one card is the ace of spades. Everyone sits in a circle and is dealt a card. The person with the ace of spades is the killer, and she or he has to "kill" everyone else in the circle by winking at them. When the killer winks at someone, that person waits a few moments and then dies a dramatic death and gets out of the circle. The killer must make sure that no one sees her or him wink except for the person she or he is trying to kill. If someone thinks she or he sees the killer at work, that person can accuse the suspected killer. If the accuser is right, the killer is caught and you start a new game. If the accuser is wrong, then the accuser has to die a dramatic death and the killer is still at large. The game ends when the killer has killed all but one person, or the killer is caught.

Games can really keep a party moving and old favorites, like Charades, are even more fun than they used to be!

QUIET GAMES

These are good for indoor parties, or for any get-together where you just want to hang out quietly with your friends.

STORIES IN A CIRCLE

Before the party, write down on separate pieces of paper all the kinds of stories you can think of—romance, western, science fiction, adventure or murder mystery—and put them in a hat. At your party, get everyone together in a circle and pick a type of story to tell. The first person starts the story. After that person has been telling the story for a while, she or he will say "Suddenly . . ." and the next person has to continue the story. The last few people should start tying up the loose ends so the last person can end the story.

TWENTY QUESTIONS

One person is "It" and thinks of a place, object or person. (The person can be fictional or real, dead or alive.) Try to pick someone or something everyone knows or has heard of. Everyone else has to discover what It is thinking of by asking twenty questions that can only be answered with a "yes" or a "no." One way to make this game easier is to stick with famous people only.

WHO KNOWS THE SONG?

Before your party, go through a dictionary or sit with your parents and come up with different words. Write each word on a separate piece of paper and put them into a hat or a bag. Divide into teams—as many as you want. Someone picks a word from the hat. For example, if the word is "happy," then each team must come up with a song that has the word "happy" in it and sing at least eight words of that song, including the selected word. Then it's the next team's turn. Teams are out when they can't come up with a song or don't know at least eight words of it.

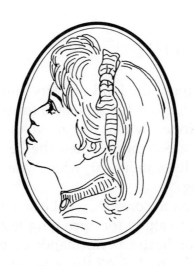

Party Preparations

"Julie, there are only two weeks left until my party," Jasmine said to her friend. "I have to write a book report and study for that awful history test. *And* I have to start cleaning the basement. What should I do first?"

CHECK IT OUT

Once you know the kind of party you want, you can start figuring out the timetable for when things have to be done—when you need to know how many people are coming, when the best time is to put up the decorations or when you should go food-shopping.

You also need to consider what else you're doing. Will you have to study for upcoming tests, rehearse for a school orchestra performance or baby-sit the night before the party? All these factors are important and will affect what you can do and when you can do it.

You might have other considerations as well—making or buying a costume for your Halloween party, making ice for cold drinks a few days before the event or shopping for special party favors.

In order to keep all these things straight, it's a good idea to have some sort of check list. With most major parties, you'll have to do a lot of advance planning, and check lists are the best tool you can use to organize your thoughts and help make everything run smoothly. Depending on how elaborate a party you're having, you might want to start making check lists a month ahead, a couple of weeks ahead or just the week before. When you feel you're really ready to organize, start jotting down the different categories of things to be taken care of before your party. Your list might look something like this:

1. Invitations/Guests
2. Food
3. Games
4. Music
5. Decorations

Then, under each category, write down what you want to do and start planning how you are going to do it. For example:

1. Invitations—Buy balloons, felt markers, envelopes and stamps by Friday. Send them out by Sunday.

Or you might want something that may not be possible. In that case, jot down the question:

4. Music—Ask Michael if I can borrow his dance tapes and cassette player. If not, see if Deirdre will let me make tapes at her house.

The more you write down, the less you have to worry about remembering—it will all be there on paper for you. And the more you plan, the less chance there is of something going wrong.

FUN, FUN, FUN IS THE NAME OF THE GAME

The whole purpose of a party is having a good time with your friends. So add "Have a good time" to your list of things to do.

In order to have a good time, just follow these basic rules:

1. Invite people you like.
2. Plan ahead and then let the party roll.
3. Plan games you like.
4. Enjoy the party you're *giving*—don't spend the party regretting that it's not quite the one you imagined.
5. Let your friends, parents and siblings help you.
6. Relax.

THE FINAL COUNTDOWN

Once the invitations are out, you probably won't need to do much more until the week before your party. If you do have something to do two weeks before your party, put that item on your calendar.

It's good to have two different types of check lists—a general one like the one above, which you keep filling in as you think of things, and a specific one for the days you'll actually be preparing for your party.

Creating a check list for two weeks before the party, one week before the party, two days before, the day before and the day of the party is a great way to stay organized. As the weeks go by, getting closer to the big day, you'll think of things to fill in. Or you might even realize you don't need to worry about certain things you thought you would.

The lists below might be helpful when making up your own list, though yours will be more specific. And remember, even if you have something listed to be done the week before your party and you can't get it done until two days before, don't get upset about it—just keep moving it over on your check list.

Sample Check List

A Week Before	Two Days Before	The Day Before
1. Finalize menu	1. Figure out what to wear	1. Decorate
2. Shop for nonfood items	2. Buy food	2. Finish last minute cleaning
3. Choose games	3. Clean	3. Do any food preparation possible
4. Finalize list of who is coming if possible	4. Get activities equipment together	4. Set up the room for the party
5. Figure out or tape music	5. Make sure everyone has directions	
	6. Have music finished	

It's good to organize your check lists so you can just go down each row and tick off each job as you do it. If you have any messy jobs on the day of your party, try to get them done as early as possible. You don't want to shower before you bring the extra chairs down from the dusty attic. And you definitely don't want to wear your favorite party clothes while you help prepare the spaghetti sauce. By focusing on what needs to be done when, you can be sure to get those messy jobs out of the way.

CHECK LIST CHECK

Check lists are supposed to make party planning easier, not more difficult, so if the lists are giving you a hard time, come up with your own method. The point is to make giving a party as simple and pleasant as possible.

And don't get too carried away making lists—sometimes making lists can take up more time than actually doing the job. Just use your list as an organizer or a reminder. Do it in whatever way is the most helpful to you—no one method is correct. So if you have a special organization technique, go right ahead and use it!

I HAVE NOTHING TO WEAR!

It's that time—the time when your closet looms larger than the Grand Canyon; when your mirror follows you everywhere, muttering that nothing looks good on you; when your brother makes sure to point out that your hair looks even worse than usual.

Sure, it's easy to write "shower and dress" on a list, but the reality of that item can be overwhelming. Choosing what to wear to your own party seems to take years if not decades of consideration and thought. King Solomon for all his wisdom would probably be useless at a time like this—what would he say, wear half of one outfit and half of another?

Yet deciding what to wear does *not* have to be the

Clothes don't have to be a drag. Just make sure you feel comfortable enough for whatever activities you have planned. And if you're really stuck for what to wear, ask a friend or a sister if you can raid her closet.

end of the world. And, no, you do *not* need to buy a new outfit. Do you know how to figure out what is appropriate, how not to go overboard and what to wear so you feel good and comfortable? Take this quick quiz and find out!

☆☆ QUICK PARTY CLOTHES ☆☆ QUIZ

1. *You're having a slumber party. You wear:*
    a. Your father's ratty old robe, hoping no one will notice the holes in the elbows.
    b. The flowered nightgown you got last year that feels really comfortable, and your blue fuzzy slippers.
    c. A sweat suit.
    d. A brand-new pair of satin pajamas.
2. *You've decided to have a dancing party. You put on:*
    a. Your ripped-up, paint-splattered jeans and an old T-shirt.
    b. A flouncy turquoise skirt, a comfortable sweater and your favorite dancing shoes.
    c. A sweat suit.
    d. A black velvet dress with rhinestones and feathers.
3. *You planned a beach party. You'll be wearing:*
    a. Cut-off shorts, a giant T-shirt and a baseball cap.
    b. Your one-piece bathing suit, a new straw hat and an extra-large pink T-shirt.
    c. A sweat suit.
    d. A gold-lamé string bikini that can't get wet.

If you chose mostly a's, you show a tendency to be underdressed or even a little sloppy. This is a party, remember? Live it up!

If you chose mostly b's, then you have a good sense of what is comfortable, what makes you look good and what's suitable for a party. Never fear—you'll be dressed exactly right.

The c answers indicate a bit of one-track-mindedness—there *are* other things to wear besides a sweat suit, you know! A little variety will go a long way.

The d answers, although they may be appropriate for a movie star, don't quite fit someone who isn't even driving yet. Besides, if you're constantly worrying about ruining your gorgeous clothes, how can you have a good time?

☆☆☆

THE KEY IS COMFORT

There are only a few things to consider when deciding what to wear if you want to feel good, look good and be comfortable. Think about what you've planned for your party. If you're going to be playing outdoor sports, a tight skirt will restrict your fun. But if it's a dancing party, then a skirt is great. And if you're going horseback riding, sandals just won't cut it—but they would be perfect for a beach party.

If you absolutely hate, hate, *hate* all your clothes, see if you can borrow something from your sister or a friend. It may not be new, but at least it'll be the first time *you're* wearing it. The party won't be a disaster and people won't hate you if you don't buy that perfect periwinkle-blue sweater that costs more than the entire party.

Party Tip

Give yourself as much time as you need to have fun getting dressed for your party. But *don't* ignore whatever else you have to do, and *don't* make your parents do everything while you're in a bubble bath.

LAST MINUTE DETAILS

Jasmine felt pressured, but she actually had enough time for everything. Her friend Julie advised her to keep a list, and so whenever Jasmine thought of something she needed to do for her party, she wrote it down. Soon, she had a pretty long list.

Since she had a book report due and a test the week of the party, Jasmine started cleaning the basement two weeks before the big day. While she cleaned, she listened to her parents' albums, deciding which songs to record on her tapes.

A week before her party, everyone had called to say they were coming. Jasmine and her father finished cleaning the basement that weekend and attached her mother's old spread to the ceiling. After making some music tapes, Jasmine focused on her test and book report for the rest of the weekend.

On Thursday afternoon, after the test and report were over, Jasmine and her mother went shopping for the food, drinks, face paints and brushes. They then put her outfit together. Jasmine decided to wear a pair of her old jeans with flowers, hearts, peace signs and stars painted on them. She wore a tie-dyed T-shirt and her mother's old suede, fringed vest. She also had a pair of moccasins. She knew she would look great and feel comfortable.

Friday night Jasmine baked the brownies and chocolate chip cookies. She also made a last-minute list for the things she had left to do on Saturday:

Saturday morning
1. Set up furniture in basement
2. Put out bowls and plates for food
3. Put out cups and bring juices and sodas downstairs
4. Change bulbs
5. Light incense (she had forgotten to do that on Friday)
6. Bring tape player and speakers downstairs
7. Make sure Dad has his videocamera ready with film

Saturday afternoon
1. Make dips
2. Bring cooler downstairs, fill with ice and put in bottles of soda
3. Cut up vegetables
4. Make lists of couples on paper

Saturday evening
1. Shower and dress
2. Make sure music tapes are downstairs
3. Bring down cheese, crackers, vegetables, brownies, cookies and candies and put them out

AN ORGANIZED OUTLOOK

Ellen felt she had to be very organized. A week before the party, she and her sister ordered a birthday cake from Ellen's favorite bakery. Ellen made up a list of what she had to do and when.

Saturday—the day before the party
1. Shop with Dad for the food, candles and flowers
2. Pick up the birthday cake
3. Set the table for lunch on Saturday night

Sunday morning
1. Make the salad
2. Make the honey/mustard mixture
3. Prepare the melons
4. Get the dessert plates ready
5. Shower
6. Get dressed

Ellen figured that she could serve the food and then she and her friends would clear the table after the meal. Because her sister had agreed to do the dishes and set the table for dessert, Ellen promised to do some of her chores during the week.

At first Ellen didn't know what she was going to wear to her party. She didn't like any of her clothes, so she asked her sister if she could raid her closet, but nothing there seemed special, either. Then one day Ellen and her sister went into a secondhand store and Ellen saw a dress that she loved. It wasn't in the best shape, but it was different, inexpensive and fit her perfectly. Wearing it, she felt grown-up and pretty.

SCOUTING IT OUT

Melissa made a master list of the different areas of her party that needed to be taken care of: Food, Location, Games, Decorations and Favors.

Two weeks before the party, Melissa and her mother scouted out Verona Park to decide exactly where her party would take place—what was the prettiest part of the park? How convenient was it to parking? Where could they set up the barbecue grill? (Most parks restrict barbecuing to certain areas of the park.) Melissa and her mother also wanted to make sure they could easily carry all the supplies to the area and Melissa needed to get enough balloons to decorate the route to the actual location of the party.

When that was settled, Melissa made a shopping list separated into food and decorations. To make things easier, Melissa's mother suggested that they shop for all the nonfood items a week before the party. Then that Thursday, Melissa and her mother would shop for the food.

One week before her party, Melissa wrote out a list for what she needed to do on the day of the party:

1. Load up the car with all the nonperishables.
2. Eat breakfast.
3. Shower and dress for the party.
4. Get the food ready to go, but keep it all in the refrigerator.

5. Go to the park and set up decorations, food, barbecue stuff and volleyball net.

For her party clothes, Melissa selected her favorite jeans, a purple-and-white striped T-shirt and her white sneakers. It wasn't a fancy outfit, but she wanted to feel comfortable and be able to run around without worrying about her clothes.

Melissa also had to make an alternate plan; she had to decide what she and her guests would do indoors in case it rained. She didn't really want to think about the possibility—the whole idea behind this party was to have it outdoors in the sunshine and warm weather—but she knew it would be better to be prepared. She and her mother got the screened-in back porch ready, so that everybody could hang out there while they had a barbecue right by the side of the house where it was protected from the rain. They also found a bunch of board games and got some records out. It wouldn't be perfect, but at least it would be a party.

They're Here!

*E*llen woke up Sunday morning feeling happy and alert. Suddenly she remembered that today was her birthday party! That's when she started getting nervous. . . .

"I DON'T WANT TO HAVE A PARTY!"

Is that you five minutes before the first guest is supposed to arrive? Don't listen to that voice—it's just your pre-party jitters speaking.

Everyone gets nervous throwing a party, and everyone goes through those last minute fears and wishes they lived in Siberia. It's normal to feel nervous; you want to have a wonderful party, and you're afraid that it might not work out. That makes perfect sense. You've worked hard and you want everyone, including yourself, to have fun. But don't worry yourself sick over what may or may not happen.

A successful party depends on you and how you feel. This doesn't mean that if you're feeling great all your friends will automatically feel great, too. But your "up" mood will have an effect on your guests and on your party. If one of your friends is in a bad mood, your being in a good one won't necessarily snap her out of it, but it will certainly help.

Even if you've planned a certain party and now either nature or circumstances has changed it, try really hard not to be too blue about it. Your friends know that you can't stop the rain, or produce a play if the one you chose closed down. They don't know about the incredible game you planned that can only be played in the swimming pool that now leaks, or the dress you wanted to buy but couldn't afford. They just know about the games they *do* play, the food you *do* serve, and the clothes you *are* wearing—they don't know or care about the might-have-beens.

If it makes you feel better, ask one of your closest friends to come over early, to hang out with you. She can help you put out those last-minute food dishes or decide which earrings you should wear. She can also reassure you and tell you that everything will be fine, and you won't be facing your first

Having a trusted friend come by early can help you shake off those dreaded pre-party jitters.

guest all alone. If nothing else, at least your attention will be on your friend a little—you won't be able to think nonstop, "This is the worst night of my life!"

Once the party actually starts, you probably won't have time to focus on your panic—you'll be too busy being with your friends, dancing, playing games and having a terrific time. And if every now and then you get nervous again, just look around at your guests and see how much they're enjoying themselves.

Party panic can make the smallest hitch look like an international disaster. Remember that parties are supposed to be *fun*, and it's hard to have fun if everything becomes a life-and-death issue. (What? You don't have potato chips with ridges? Call off the party!) Most things that seem like catastrophes before or during a party really aren't. It's only that the hostess is a mass of nerves.

Do you have party poise? Take the quiz below and see.

☆☆ PARTY POISE QUIZ ☆☆

1. *You and your mother planned a lunch party for your friends. But your mother came down with a terrible cold, and you know you can't make the baked chicken and everything else alone. You:*
   a. Postpone the party.
   b. Order in Chinese food.
   c. Get really angry at your mother for ruining your party.

d. Convince your mother to get out of bed
      and help you.
2. *You made dance tapes for your party, but hardly
   anybody is dancing. A friend of yours asks if he can
   put on one of his tapes. You say:*
      a. No, and try playing a game instead.
      b. No, letting your party die out.
      c. Yes, and join in as your friends begin to
         dance and the party takes off.
      d. Yes, and then sulk when your friends
         dance to his tape.
3. *At your slumber party, you planned to serve chocolate
   fondue at midnight, but the fondue has turned into
   cement and the pound cake is stale. Your great feast
   has turned to famine. You:*
      a. Ask your mom if you can call out for
         pizza.
      b. Tell everyone your party is over.
      c. Make a joke and encourage everyone to
         eat the food anyway.
      d. Get sulky and ignore the fact that your
         friends are hungry.
4. *The boy you have a crush on comes to your party, but
   he seems to be paying more attention to another girl
   than to you. You:*
      a. Tell that girl to go home.
      b. Pretend you don't care, but be secretly
         miserable throughout the party.
      c. Realize that you can't always get what
         you want, and find someone else to
         dance with.
      d. Insist that he dance with you or be your
         partner for one of the games.
5. *Your younger sister won't leave you and your friends*

alone, even though she was supposed to go to a friend's house. She wants to watch and play everything. You:

- a. Complain to your mother and ask her to get rid of your sister.
- b. Let her join in for one game, then let her stay when you realize she isn't ruining your party.
- c. Scream at your sister no matter what she does.
- d. Ignore her totally.

6. *You're playing charades, one of your favorite games, but it seems as if your guests aren't really enjoying it. You:*

- a. Continue to play it for as long as you had planned.
- b. Ask how many want to continue playing and then follow the majority.
- c. Stop playing charades and refuse to do anything else.
- d. Sulk because no one likes the games you like.

7. *Your friends seem to be eating more than you thought they would and the food is running out. You:*

- a. Panic and tell some of your closest friends to stop eating.
- b. Tell your mother, and then leave her to deal with it.
- c. Do nothing—you're not hungry anyway.
- d. Tell your mother and see if someone can run to the store and buy more food.

8. *It's your party, and everyone but you seems to be having a great time. You:*

- a. Pretend that you are.

80

b. Tell everyone it's over and then go up to your room.
c. Tell your best friend and see if she can cheer you up or tell you what's wrong.
d. Mope in the kitchen.

9. *You're throwing a party so your camp friends can meet your school friends, but no one is mixing. You have these great games planned, but everyone is holding back. You:*

a. Physically move everyone into teams.
b. Spend your party running back and forth between the two groups, feeling miserable.
c. Ask your closest friends in each group to help you get a game started.
d. Ask your mother to help.

10. *You planned all these great decorations, but when you finally got them up you thought they looked stupid. You:*

a. Pull them all down before your guests arrive and spend the whole party apologizing for not having any decorations.
b. Revise what you had planned and use only some of the decorations.
c. Leave it all up and feel secretly embarrassed through the party.
d. Panic and stay really angry throughout the whole party.

Answers:

1.	2.	3.	4.	5.
a. 2	a. 2	a. 3	a. 0	a. 2
b. 3	b. 1	b. 0	b. 2	b. 3
c. 0	c. 3	c. 2	c. 3	c. 0
d. 0	d. 0	d. 1	d. 1	d. 1

6.	a. 2	7.	a. 1	8.	a. 2	9.	a. 1	10.	a. 1
	b. 3		(b.) 2		b. 0		b. 0		b. 3
	(c.) 0		c. 0		(c.) 3		(c.) 3		(c.) 2
	d. 1		d. 3		d. 1		d. 2		d. 0

Add up your scores and then see where you fit.

0–9 *Party Pooper.* Yes, things are going wrong, but it doesn't mean that the party has to stop or you have to be so upset you can't face anyone. Don't give up on your own party. Look around you—most of your friends are probably having a good time. Just mellow out and you'll have fun, too.

10–16 *Party Pest.* You're doing somewhat better than the Party Pooper—at least the party is still going on. You're someone who has to have your own way all the time, and if something doesn't go exactly your way, you'll sulk or pout. Or else you remind everyone about what went wrong instead of enjoying what's happening right now. Try not to sink your own party. Having things done your way isn't important, but everyone having fun *is.*

17–24 *Party Professional.* You know how to throw a party and do all the right things—*except* have a good time yourself and not fall apart when something goes wrong. On the outside you look like you're having fun, but your best friend can probably tell that you're upset about the game that never got off the ground. Take heart: If everybody else is having a good time, you can too!

25–30 *Party Princess.* You've got it all. When something goes wrong, you keep your cool, handle it yourself or get help and continue to have a good time. You might get a bit frazzled, but you know how to keep your party poise and have fun.

☆☆☆

JUMP-STARTING YOUR PARTY

Everyone is there and you've greeted all your guests. How do you get your party started? How do you make sure there's always enough food available, start the games and talk to your friends all at the same time? You ask for help—from your parents and friends, and maybe even your brothers and sisters.

Your parents will probably help you take care of the food. You can even get your younger siblings to bring food in whenever more is needed. It will make them feel like part of the party, and it will give you one less thing to worry about.

The key to managing a party is not doing everything yourself. Get help so you don't have to think about everything. How can you possibly be involved in a game if you have to worry about putting candles on your birthday cake? Before the party starts, plan with your family as to who will do what job. Perhaps you might be in charge of activities, music and drinks. Your father can handle the food and your mother can take pictures. Your best friend can help by being enthusiastic about playing each game or being one of the first people to dance. That's something best friends are great at—being there to help as much as possible.

1. Candles—aside from those on a cake or at a formal dinner party—are not a good idea. You want to have fun at your party, not worry about having a bonfire in your living room.
2. Active games are fun, but if some of your guests are getting too rowdy, try to cool things down yourself or ask a parent to help.
3. If you're having a party any place other than your home, make sure everyone stays together and that everyone is comfortable with the activity. Also, alert your friends to possible dangers.
4. If anything looks as though it could be dangerous, get your parents or some other grownup *immediately.*

ARE YOU HAVING FUN?

How do you know if you're having fun, if your party is a success or if your guests are having fun?

First of all, it's easy to figure out if *you're* having fun—just see how you feel inside! You're probably a mix of excitement, nervousness and happiness. Your nerves may not calm down until after the party, but you can still have a fantastic time!

Are your friends having fun? Take a look around you every so often. Are they smiling, active, involved in whatever is going on? If you're playing a noisy game, is there noise? If it's a quieter game, is everyone participating?

Most importantly, if you're having fun, that will radiate out and your friends can't help but pick up on it. So have a great time—it's your party!

SUCCESS STORIES

Melissa absolutely loved her party. The weather stayed beautiful until the very end of the party when the wind picked up, but that made kite-flying a breeze. The potluck picnic was great, and the ribbons and balloons made everything festive. Aside from the volleyball net falling down every now and then, the party was a great success.

Ellen was sure her party was ruined when her father's car conked out—how would they all get to the play? Not panicking, Ellen's father called the mother of one of the girls and found a fast replacement.

After that everything went smoothly. The lunch was delicious and everyone loved the play. Ellen was sure this was the best birthday ever.

Disaster might have struck when they returned from the play: Ellen's sister had become so involved in her research paper that she forgot to do the dishes or set the table for dessert. At first Ellen was embarrassed, then she asked some of her friends to help her set the table. Her friends were more than glad to help. After that, the party was great.

Jasmine knew her party was fabulous. The face-painting went well and everyone danced, even the shyest boys and girls in her class. But at one point, Jasmine noticed Michael and Jeff trying to pull the

Indian spread off the ceiling. Soon, she knew, the other boys would join in.

She ran up to the kitchen quickly and asked her father to come and videotape everyone dancing. She knew the boys would stop fooling around once her father came back into the room, and she was right.

The party lasted longer than she expected because everyone wanted to see the video. By the end of the evening, Jasmine wished she could have a party every month!

The Party's Over

Melissa looked around the picnic site. Most of the leftover food had been put away, but the ribbons and balloons still had to come down, the barbecue grill and the volleyball net had to be dismantled and everything had to be packed into her mother's car. The place was a mess: It had been a great party, but cleaning up was going to be a major chore.

CALLING THE CLEANUP CREW

Cleanup can be fun. You don't buy that, huh? Well, how about *bearable*?

Seriously, if throughout the party you pick up empty bottles, cups, plates and napkins and throw them away, you'll have an easier time cleaning afterward. Also, if garbage bags or garbage cans are available, some of your guests may take the hint and throw some of their garbage away themselves.

That doesn't mean you should get obsessed with neatness—don't grab a can of soda out of a friend's hand before she's finished drinking in order to throw it away. Cleaning up during the party is a small job you can give your younger sister or brother (then you might include them in a game or give them a party favor as a thank-you).

Remember, asking people to be neat and even to help clean up is not rude. If you're having your friends over for lunch, feel free to ask them to bring their plates and the leftover food into the kitchen. You might even ask your closer friends to stay a little while longer and help clean up, knowing that you'll repay the favor when they have parties.

PICKING UP THE PIECES

Ellen had a lot of dishes to wash after everyone left, since her sister had left everything out and dirty. Her best friend Danielle stayed and helped dry. Aside from washing and putting all the dishes away, she didn't have much more to do. Ellen persuaded her sister to help her put all the extra chairs away and straighten up the living room a bit, since she'd missed most of her part of the deal.

Melissa didn't actually have much to clean up either. After having such a great time at her party, she really dreaded cleanup. But her friend Diane stayed and helped. Although the job looked tremendous before they started, it really didn't take long at all.

Jasmine, on the other hand, had a lot of work to do. She had to return the pillows, lamps and Indian spread to where they belonged, as well as clean up the mess. (The floor was very sticky from spilled soda.) She also had to put away the extra food.

It was late and Jasmine was tired. But she knew everything would only look worse in the morning, so she started right away, with her parents' help. After they finished cleaning up most of the mess, they decided that Jasmine could wait to put away the decorations until the next day.

THANK YOU, THANK YOU, THANK YOU

As your guests left, they probably all said "Thank you for a great party," or "Thanks, I had a great time."

There might be a few people *you* should thank as well:

1. *Your parents*—They let you have the party. Did they help out? Were they understanding about the type of party you wanted?

2. *Your siblings*—Did they help you? Did they stay out of your way? Were they on their extra-special good behavior?
3. *Your close friends*—Did some of your friends help you plan the party, organize the games and clean up afterward?
4. *All your other friends*—Did they bring you presents? And if they did, is a phone call enough to say thank you or should you send out thank-you notes?
5. *Yourself*—Did you thank yourself for giving such a great party and being such a good hostess?

On a similar note, have you congratulated yourself for all the planning and work you did? You should. It's not easy to give a party—it takes a lot of organization and imagination. That's why there are professional party-planners. People hire them because they know how difficult it is to plan a party. So congratulate yourself and thank yourself for a great job!

STILL LATER

You might feel some post-party blues. That's perfectly natural. For weeks now you've been gearing yourself up for "The Party" and now it's over. What have you got to look forward to now? Geography class?

If those post-party blues hit, don't worry—they'll be gone before you know it. You'll have something fun planned for the next weekend, or you'll try out for the school play, or you'll get involved in your favorite sport. Maybe there's even another party you're invited to.

GOING TO A PARTY

It shouldn't be so difficult to decide what to wear to somebody else's party, but sometimes it seems like an impossible chore. If the host or hostess tells you what kind of party it is—a beach party, a dance party, a hanging-out party, a costume party—that will give you some idea as to how to dress.

Let's say you're invited to tea with Prince Charles and Princess Diana. What do you wear? Obviously, a ladylike dress. But if it's a baseball game in the local stadium in August, you wear shorts, a T-shirt, a baseball cap and plenty of sunscreen. Or say you're going to your stuffy great-aunt's: You'll wear a pretty dress, your best shoes and the necklace she gave you.

And you say you never know what to wear? Of course you do!

Sometimes costume parties are actually easier, because although it might be a problem getting a costume together, at least you know what you are looking for.

"But what if it's just a regular party?" you ask. "What do I wear then?"

Why not ask the hostess what kind of party she has in mind or what she's going to wear? While the party-giver sometimes dresses up more than the guests, you can get a pretty good idea of the type of party it's going to be from what the hostess plans to wear.

Finally, go for what makes you comfortable. If it's the kind of party where you can wear either jeans or a skirt, and you're more comfortable in jeans, wear jeans.

THE ART OF PARTY-GOING

So you've been invited to a party and you know exactly what to wear, but you don't know how to act. Relax—you survived your own party, didn't you? The idea is more or less the same for going to someone else's party: Just try to relax, be yourself, and you'll have a great time.

This is easy advice to give, but it's not always so easy to follow. How do you do it? By thinking about other people at the party and not worrying about the impression you're making on them. Concentrate on the guests, the games and the food and soon you'll find that you're not self-conscious at all. You're having fun just like everybody else.

You might plan to go with a friend so there's at least one person with whom you feel comfortable. Then hang out with the friends you know best. And remember, the other guests are your friends, too— or they could be if you give them the chance. If you don't know some of the people, go up to them and introduce yourself. You may discover that they don't know many of the other kids, either, and they'll probably be grateful to you for your friendly gesture.

If you still feel uncomfortable, that's okay, too. Just because it's a party doesn't mean you can

Help your host out when you go to someone else's party by introducing yourself to unfamiliar faces. You could make some fantastic new friends and have a wonderful time!

automatically flick a switch and turn on a party mood. But if you focus on other people rather than on yourself, you'll probably end up having a good time. Think about the hostess and remember how important it was to *you* that your guests enjoy themselves at your party. So for her sake, try to have fun.

Of course, if you feel uncomfortable or nervous about any of the activities your host or hostess has planned, you don't have to participate. But be pleasant about it—don't just sit in a corner and sulk!

Pick a Party—Any Party

*I*t's great to give a party and know that you've worked out the details all by yourself. But what if you don't have the time or any good ideas? In this chapter you will find complete party plans, which you can use as ideas for your own party. You can follow one whole plan from top to bottom, you can pick and choose bits and pieces from each or you can just use them for inspiration, getting your own ideas as you read them. However you choose to read this chapter, we hope you have lots of fun!

SLUMBER PARTY

A slumber party is one of the few times you're *expected* to stay up late and giggle and talk with your friends!

INVITATIONS

If you like to sew, make little pillows out of white fabric and write the invitations on them, using a pen that writes on material. Or take whatever kind of paper you like and fold it to make a card. On the cover, write "I'm having a slumber party!" and then write the following inside:

Where: At Patricia's, 395 Woodland Avenue
When: Friday night, July 18th from 7 P.M. till Saturday morning at 11 A.M.
R.S.V.P: 555–9583
Bring: A sleeping bag, slippers and a robe (it's cold at my house).

FOOD

These are traditional slumber-party foods, but if you don't like them, create your own menu. You might want to add something healthy and non-fattening such as fruit, juices or fresh vegetables.

For the evening:

- ✪ *Pizza*
- ✪ *Popcorn*
- ✪ *Ice cream*
- ✪ *Soda*

For the morning:

- ✪ *Waffles or French toast, fruit and juice*

DECORATIONS

You don't need much in the way of decorations. Make sure there are a lot of pillows and blankets around the room to give your party that cozy feeling.

THINGS TO DO

- ✪ *Rent a movie*
- ✪ *Stories in a Circle**
- ✪ *Dance (have some dance music on hand)*
- ✪ *Pillow fights—Just make sure there's nothing in the room that can get broken*
- ✪ *Wrap-the-Mummy**
- ✪ *Lip-synching your favorite songs*
- ✪ *Killer**

Note: Games like Truth or Dare usually end up being hurtful and not fun.

---

*See Chapter Six for the rules of the game.

REVERSAL PARTY

There are many different kinds of reversal parties. One kind is having a luau in the winter or a winter party in the summer. This reversal party is a *totally* backward party.

INVITATIONS

Write the invitations out in mirror writing. One way to do this is to write the invitation out normally, stand it up in front of a mirror and trace the mirror image on tracing paper. It could read something like this:

It's the Great Backward Birthday Party!
I'm a year younger—Help me celebrate!

Place: Jo's house at 401 Germantown Rd.
Time: Saturday, February 21, 7:30–10:30 P.M.
R.S.V.P. 555–2323

You must wear your clothes backward, inside out or in the wrong order. Be prepared to walk backward, talk backward, even eat backward.

FOOD

Make sure you eat dessert first and then the regular food.

- ✪ Upside-down cake
- ✪ Upside-down hamburgers (bottom roll on top)
- ✪ Salad

DECORATIONS

Whatever room you're in, try to turn everything around so it is backward. Make the chairs face the wall, the pictures face away from everyone, turn the rug over and so on.

THINGS TO DO

- ✪ From the moment your friends step through the door, they have to walk backward. Say goodbye when they enter and hello when they leave.
- ✪ Have a fashion show for the new reversal look. Make sure everyone walks backward down the runway.
- ✪ Have a backward talking contest—who can say their names or other words backward, and then who can say entire sentences backward.
- ✪ Sing songs backward.
- ✪ Open the presents first.
- ✪ Take pictures of everyone's backs.

FAVORS

- ✪ Upside-down cupcakes
- ✪ Invisible ink pens
- ✪ The last book in a series
- ✪ Black paper and a silver pen

HALLOWEEN PARTY

INVITATIONS

Cut out a black cat shape. Decorate one side with glitter or different-shaped, small pieces of colored construction paper. On the other side, use a silver or gold marker and write out the invitation:

Calling all spooks, goblins and witches—
Come to Andi's Scariest Halloween Party!

Where: 271 Mira Vista
When: Saturday, October 30 from 8–11 P.M.
R.S.V.P. 555–5163
Wear a Costume!

FOOD

- *Pumpkin pie or bread*
- *Candy corn*
- *Hot cider with cinnamon sticks*

DECORATIONS

- *Orange and black streamers and balloons*
- *Spider webs (You can buy fake spider webs or use string to make your own)*
- *Low lighting*
- *Pumpkins or jack-o'-lanterns*

MUSIC

- ✪ *Organ music/any eerie music*
- ✪ *Dance music*

THINGS TO DO

- ✪ *Bob for apples*
- ✪ *Carve pumpkins*
- ✪ *Wrap-the-Mummy**
- ✪ *Tell ghost stories*
- ✪ *If you have an extra room and the time beforehand, you can create a mini haunted house for your guests to go through*
- ✪ *Have a contest for the scariest, the most original, the prettiest or the strangest costume (be sure to tell your guests on the invitation that there will be a costume contest)*
- ✪ *If it's a small party and it's on Halloween, you could all go out trick-or-treating together*

FAVORS

- ✪ *Apples*
- ✪ *Little rubber skeletons or spiders*
- ✪ *A decorated bag for trick-or-treating*

*See Chapter Six for the rules of this game.

HORSEBACK-RIDING PARTY

INVITATIONS

Make the invitation in the shape of a boot or a horse. Stick a few pieces of hay in each envelope so that your guests will get the feeling of a stable right away.

Come join Harriet for her birthday on a wild ride!

Where: Meet at Silver Spurs Riding School
       393 Woodland Avenue
When: Saturday, September 5 before 1 P.M.
      After riding for an hour, we'll mosey over
      to Harriet's for some grub until 5 P.M.
R.S.V.P. 555–7989 by August 31
Wear: Jeans and sturdy, old shoes or boots. Cowboy hats optional.

All kinds of horses are available at Silver Spurs, from spirited steeds to gentle ponies.

Before you even send out the invitations call the stable to see if they accept groups and if so, if there's a limit to how many people can be in a party. After you learn how much it costs per person, ask what happens if someone cancels at the last minute—do you still have to pay for that person? What happens if it rains? What kind of horses do they have? You'll probably have additional questions of your own. You might have to decide if you're going to go on a

Horsing around? It's a great idea for a theme party and a guaranteed terrific time!

trail with a guide or just stay in the corral. Find out when you have to let the stable know the number of people in your group and ask for R.S.V.P.'s a few days earlier than that on the invitation.

Note: This is an expensive party to give, so if you are on a tight budget it's probably not a good choice.

FOOD

- ✪ *Hamburgers and hot dogs*
- ✪ *Deli food*
- ✪ *Fresh vegetables*
- ✪ *Potato salad*
- ✪ *If it's a birthday party, have a cake in the shape of a horse or a boot*
- ✪ *If you go to a restaurant, try to pick one that has a western feel to it*

DECORATIONS AND MUSIC

If your family or friends have camping equipment, you can use that for serving and eating to add that rustic, western atmosphere. Play country-western music in the background.

FAVORS

- ✪ *String ties*
- ✪ *Bandannas*
- ✪ *Horse or cow candles*
- ✪ *Little china cows or horses*

FANTASY PARTY

A fantasy party is a very special kind of costume party where everyone dresses up as something out of their wildest dreams. You can either plan it so that everyone dresses up to suit *your* imagination—in other words, if you love mermaids and the underwater world, then everyone would have to come dressed appropriately for that—or you can have each of your friends come dressed as her own fantasy, so you'll have a room filled with strange and exotic people. Fantasy or costume parties are also a great excuse to wear clothing you don't usually get to wear. You might not be able to think of a particular person you've always wanted to be, but you might have always wanted to dress in a certain way. Here's your chance! Let your imagination run wild!

INVITATIONS

Buy or make plain half-masks—masks that only cover your eyes. Decorate the part that shows with markers, glitter, feathers and any other material you have. On the back part, write out your invitation. If you want your friends to wear the masks, you'll have to either write your invitation out on something else or cover the ink with some sort of plastic. You don't want your friends to wear your invitation on their faces!

For Girls Only
Live out your fantasies

Come to Shari's for tea on Saturday, April 11th
from 2:30 to 5:00 P.M.
Come dressed as your fantasy—
A royal princess, a rock star, an Arabian
dancer
Shari's palace: 8 Manger Road
R.S.V.P. 555–4077

Come dressed or bring your outfit with you.

FOOD

- ✪ *Serve a tea with regular tea or herb tea. If some of your guests don't like tea, serve juice or hot chocolate.*
- ✪ *Prepare cucumber sandwiches—thin slices of cucumbers on buttered white bread with the crusts cut off. Two slices of bread can make four small sandwiches.*
- ✪ *Buy or make a pound cake.*
- ✪ *If you have time, make scones and serve them with heavy cream and jam*
- ✪ *Or buy some fancy pastries from a local bakery*

THINGS TO DO

- ✪ *Have a real tea—all very proper. Make sure you pour for your guests.*
- ✪ *Have everyone act as their fantasy person for a certain amount of time. Have a show in which everyone models their outfits. Each model can tell a little bit about her fantasy character, her likes and dislikes, who some of her favorite people are and so on.*

106

- ✪ *You can certainly have dancing—even Florence Nightingale must have danced.*
- ✪ *Definitely take lots of pictures. Ask your friends to take pictures, too, so you can make sure you have some of yourself.*

FAVORS

- ✪ *An ornamental teacup*
- ✪ *Costume jewelry—an "emerald" ring, "diamond" earrings and so on*
- ✪ *A magic wand, bought or decorated by you*
- ✪ *A key chain with a picture that relates to your personal theme, such as a unicorn, a mermaid or whatever*

PAINT YOUR OWN T-SHIRT PARTY

You can plan a party around a creative activity that takes place either in your home or elsewhere. You can even have a party in which someone comes in and teaches a skill to your guests, but you'll probably need to buy the necessary materials ahead of time.

For a T-shirt party, you'll need to buy 100% cotton T-shirts and paint you can use on clothes. Some paints go on flat and smoothly on the cloth, while others stand out, creating a 3-D effect. You might also want to get glitter and studs. Don't forget the brushes!

INVITATIONS

Come to Sarah's Design-Your-Own-Clothes Party

Saturday, December 11th from 2 to 4 P.M.
17 Deerfield Road
R.S.V.P. 555–2334 by December 4th and tell me
what size T-shirt you wear!

FOOD

❂ *After creating your T-shirt masterpieces, serve a lunch of sloppy Joes or hero sandwiches with all the trimmings of potato chips, pickles and salad.*

❂ *If it's really cold out, you might want to have some hot soup.*

DECORATIONS

Just getting the room ready for painting should be "decoration" enough. Make sure you have enough flat surfaces for everyone to work on, and that the furniture and floor are covered well enough so any spilled paint won't cause a major catastrophe. You might want to put up some balloons and art posters to add some creative party atmosphere.

Play music, but not too loudly—you don't want to disturb anyone's artistic mood.

THINGS TO DO

- *Paint T-shirts, of course. It might be helpful if a parent explains how to use the paint, put on the glitter and studs, and, if possible, how to fix a mistake. Each person should have at least one brush, if not two of different sizes. (Some fabric paints come in squeeze bottles so you don't need a brush, but brushes are good for creating different effects.) Supply pencils or markers if any of your guests wants to first sketch and then paint.*
- *After you've had lunch and the shirts have had a chance to dry, put on a fashion show so everyone can model their creations. Give out prizes, making sure everyone wins one. Some possible categories are Most Colorful, Most Artistic, Cutest, Most Abstract and so on. Take pictures or videotape the show so everyone can see how they look.*
- *Dance, play a few rounds of Killer*, hang out.*

FAVORS

Everyone has her own beautiful T-shirt to take home as a favor.

A PARTY PARTY

Are you in the mood for a party with no themes and no costumes? Do you just want to get together with your friends and hang out? What you're in the mood for is a *party* party!

*See Chapter Six for the rules of this game.

INVITATIONS

Go through magazines and find phrases that match the mood of the party you want to give such as "Something big is happening," "Come together," "Entertain on a grand scale" and so on. Cut these phrases out, and tape or paste them on a blank white sheet. Add all the important information and make copies. You can fold these 8½" × 11" sheets in thirds, tape them shut and address and mail them.

Please come to my party:
It's on Saturday, March 5 from 8 to 11:30 P.M.
At Rebecca's—463 Rotary Avenue
R.S.V.P. 555–2168 by February 26th

Bring your favorite group game

FOOD

- ✪ *Place chips, pretzels and candies throughout the room.*
- ✪ *Buy some deli food such as corned beef, turkey and pickles, and make potato salad. Put out rolls and slices of rye and pumpernickel bread with mustard, catsup and mayonnaise so everyone can make the kind of sandwich he or she likes.*

DECORATIONS

Now's the time to find those Christmas lights—multicolored and blinking or whatever you have—or see if you can borrow some. The night before the party, tape the lights around the doorway of the "party" room, create a design on the wall or string some across the ceiling. Make sure they won't fall during the party and get broken. If that isn't enough lighting, use lamps instead of the overhead light.

Take big, black plastic garbage bags and cut them open into rectangles. Tape them on a wall—but get your parents' permission first! Cut out stars from aluminum foil and tape them onto the black plastic. With the dim lighting from the Christmas lights and lamps, the stars should shine nicely against the black wall.

THINGS TO DO

Play everyone's game or as many as you can. Ask the person who brought the game to explain it to the group. You might want to know ahead of time what games everyone is bringing so no two people bring the same game. Or you just might want to wing it. Make sure to leave time for eating and dancing. Some back-up games and activities are Killer* and Paper Bag Dramatics*—both will be lots of fun with the subdued lighting.

*See Chapter Six for the rules of these games.

The Final Secret Ingredient

You now know practically everything about how to give a party, from invitations to cleanup.

There's just one more item that is as important as or more important than anything else: The key to giving a great party, the one thing you must do in order for it to be a success . . . Make sure you *have fun.*

Whether you're giving a small party for four, or a huge one for forty-four, enjoy it. The whole purpose

The most important part of any party is to relax, enjoy yourself and have a super time!

of a party is that you and your friends will have a good time.

Even if something goes wrong at the party—the food table collapses, it rains on your beach party or your younger brother sticks his face in the cake—your party can still be a success. And you can learn from whatever goes wrong so you'll know what to do—or what not to do—at your next party. Because you *will* give more parties and the more you have, the easier they get. For the next one, you'll know how to reinforce the legs of the table. You'll know not to plan a beach party in April. You'll know not to leave your little brother alone with the cake.

No matter what happens at your party, it'll still be great. Because it will be *your* party and all *your* friends will be there doing what *you* want to do. They'll be laughing and talking and having a great time all because of *you*. So let that warm glow of their friendship make you happy, and relax and enjoy yourself.

Whether this is your first party or your sixth or your sixtieth, send out those invitations, start the music playing and get ready to have a ball!